SCHIRMER'S LIBRARY OF MUSICAL CLASSICS

Vol. 2003

FRANZ SCHUBERT

Dances

For Piano

ISBN 978-0-7935-3537-8

G. SCHIRMER, *Inc.*

CONTENTS

"Dancing was so much the rage that on the Thursday before Carnival Sunday of 1821, for instance, sixteen hundred balls took place in a single night." So wrote Otto Erich Deutsch, the biographer of Franz Schubert and cataloguer of his works. The city where people danced in such numbers was Vienna, the capital of Austria at the time of Franz Schubert (1797–1828).

Schubert was a true Viennese, and his life was engulfed by things Viennese: the woods and the parks, theaters and churches, wine and pastries—and, of course, the dance. Schubert, in the company of his many artistic friends, frequently played dance music at the piano for their listening (and sometimes, dancing) enjoyment. It was his habit to improvise dance tunes, and when a particular piece impressed the young composer as worthy of preservation, he would write it down. Some 400 of these dances—Waltzes, Ländler, Deutsche, Ecossaises, Minuets—are Schubert's legacy to lovers of dance music.

The names which these dances bear do not necessarily reflect differences among the various types, except that the Ecossaises, the Galops, and the Cotillon are the only pieces in duple meter. There is ample evidence that Schubert himself would call the same dance by a different name on different occasions and that publishers felt no compunction about altering the name of a dance. In most instances, the publishers grouped Schubert's dances into convenient sets for publication. It appears that Schubert did not mind letting the publishers have their way with the 166 dances which were published, in seven sets, during his lifetime. In 1864, Johannes Brahms published an edition of twelve Ländler (D 790) as opus posthumous 171.

Still, the titles Schubert actually used on his manuscripts deserve some consideration. This new edition of the Dances offers the performer an opportunity to conveniently examine all the examples of each dance genre. The Minuet, introduced in the 17th century, is the most elegant of the dance types. In triple meter and stately tempo, it is often coupled with a contrasting section called a Trio. Probably derived from the *allemande,* the Deutscher Tanz, or simply Deutsche (German Dance), was a country dance which gained popularity in the late 18th century in Austria and the neighboring southern portion of Germany. It is a rather quick dance in triple meter performed by couples. The designation Deutscher Tanz was eventually replaced by the more familiar term Waltz.

The Waltz, Schubert's and Vienna's favorite dance type, evolved from the Deutscher Tanz into a quicker dance during the first half of the 19th century. By the end of the century, Johann Strauss' famed waltzes became the signature of Vienna. Couples facing each other and holding each other closely turned and swirled to the waltz's 3/4 time, as more prudish onlookers gasped. Adhering to the more relaxed pace and bucolic character of the Deutscher Tanz, the Ländler might be considered a slow waltz. The Ländler became an ethnic dance of Austria (employed by Gustav Mahler and Anton Bruckner in their Symphonies) whereas the Waltz spread to all the music centers of Europe and the United States. The term Wiener Deutsche (Viennese German Dances), used but once by Schubert, reveals the fifteen year old composer proudly crediting the city of his birth as the spiritual source of these, his first, essays in dance composition.

The Ecossaise, a type of contredanse (a lively dance movement in duple meter), was popular in Vienna in the early 19th century. Its name suggests a link to Scotland, but musically there is none. The Galop, another fast dance in 2/4 time, was often the last dance at a ball. Also common as the finale of a ball was the Cotillon, which, like its cousin the Quadrille, used a succession of musical dance genres, such as the Waltz and the Galop, to bring the night's entertainment to a rousing conclusion.

Schubert's Dances for the piano are the product of a fun-loving, middle-class, youthful, non-virtuoso musical genius who vividly captured the spirit and pulse of his native Vienna.

—L. MICHAEL GRIFFEL

36 Waltzes

FRANZ SCHUBERT, Op. 9a
D 365

4.
p
cresc.
5.
p
f
6.
7.

8.
9.
10.
mf
p
f
dimin.
cresc.

11.
mf
12.
f
mf
p
pp
sf
cresc.
13.
14.

mf
f
p
15.
16.
p
17.
p
f
fz
18.
f
dimin.
p
cresc.
dimin.
p

19.
p
cresc.
f
p
20.
ff
p
ff
p
21.
p
mf
p
1.
2.
22.
p
1.
2.

1.
2.
23.
24.
cresc.
25.
cresc.

26.
f
p
cresc.
27.
28.
mf
29.

30.
31.

32.
p
cresc.
f
pp
cresc.
f
33.
p
pp
pp
f

34.
pp
poco cresc.
p
cresc.
f
sf
35.
fp
36.
mf

16 Waltzes and Ecossaises

Op. 18a
D 145

2.
p
3.
ff
sf
sf
sf
sf
mf
1.
2.

4.
mf
pp
5.
pp
cresc.
mf
p
mf
p
pp
mf
1.
2.
6.
p
sf
sf

sf
sf
p
7.
p
fp
1.
2.
8.
p
cresc.
fp
mf
cresc.
sf
mf
1.
2.

9.

10.

11.

Ecossaises

18 German Dances and Ecossaises

Op. 33
D 783

4.
f
sf
cresc.
5.
p
mf
6.
ff
7.
Ped.

8.
mf
sf
sf
p
f
p
f
9.
fp
fp
ten.
ten.
mf
cresc.
f
ff
1.
2.
10.
pp
mf
cresc.
p
p
decresc.
11.
f
sf
sf
p

12
13.
14.
1.
2.
f
p
p
f
ff
fp
sf
sf
mf
pp
cresc.
cresc.
cresc.

15.

mf *cresc.* *decresc.* *pp*

p *f* *p*

16.

ff *sf* *sf* *sf* *ff* *ff*

ff

Ecossaises

1.

p *sf* *fp* *ff*

legato

sf

2.

f *sf*

12 Valses Sentimentales

from Op. 50
D 779

f
p
4.
p
mf
1.
2.
5.
p
dolce

mf
p
1.
2.
6.
p
f
sf
ff
7.
p
f

8.
9.
10.

11.
p
ff
p
12.
f
sf
sf
sf
sf
ff
p
f
mf

18 Ländler and Ecossaises

Homage to the Fair Ladies of Vienna

Op. 67
D 365

4.
5.
stacc. sempre
6.

pp
cresc.
f
p
f
1.
2.
7.
p
mf
f
p
8.
p
pp
mf
f

9.

p *f*

p *cresc.* *f*

10.

pp

mf *fp*

11.

p

f *pp*

dim.

12.
p
cresc.
p
13.
p
cresc.
f
p
f
p
f
14.
pp
sempre legato
decresc.
1.
2.

15.

16.

Ecossaises

1.

2.

12 Valses Nobles

Op. 77
D 969

p
cresc.
p
decresc.
pp
dim.
ff
cresc.
8
4.
p
1.
2.
8
5.
f
sf
sf
sf
p

6.
7.

8.
p
f
sf
pp
9.
ff
cresc.
10.
p legato

cresc.
p
11.
pf
f
ff
12.
f
ff
p
f
ff

12 Waltzes of Graz

Op. 91a
D 924

4.

p

f

fz

fz

p

5.

p

cresc.

decresc.

1. 2.

6.

f

345

p

1. 2.

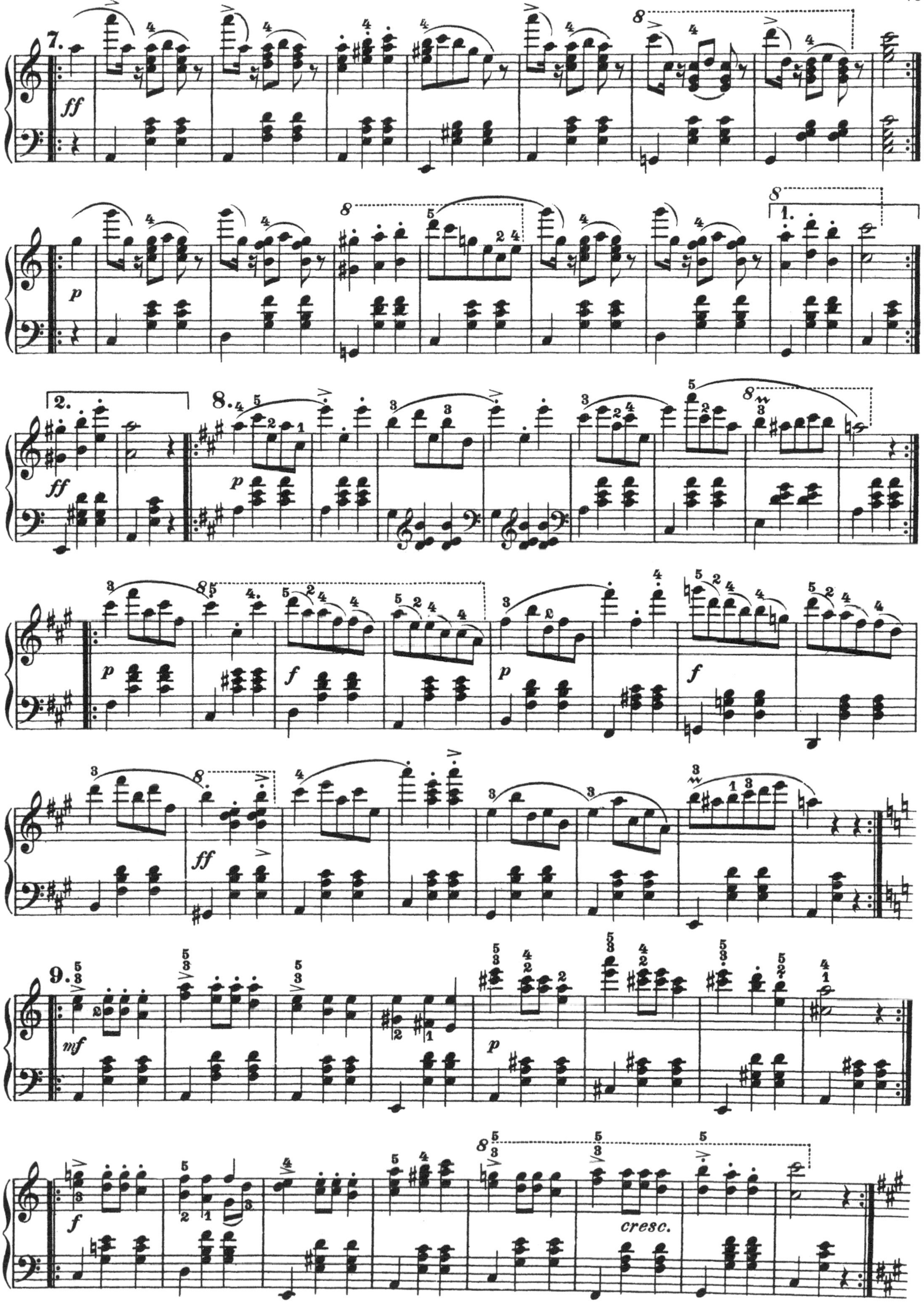
7.
ff
p
1.
2.
ff
8.
p
p
f
p
f
ff
9.
mf
p
f
cresc.

10.
11.
cresc.

mf
p
cresc.
f
12.
p
f
p
f
p
cresc.
ff
p
cresc.
f
decresc.
p
f
p
f
p
cresc.
ff

13 Last Waltzes

from Op. 127
D 146

3.
Trio
D.C.

4.
ff
Trio
p
D.C.
5.
ff
sf
sf

p
ff
sf
ff
p
Trio
pp dolce
D.C.

6.
Trio

sf

D.C.

7.

ff

ff

decresc.

p

ff

Trio

pp

mf

pp

D.C.

8.
9.
10.

11.
f
sf
sf
sf
sf
sf
p
sf
sf
sf
sf
f
12.
pp
13.
pp

Waltz

D 844

8 Ländler

from Op. 171
D 146

Alla tedesca

fz
fz
fp
pp
cresc.
fz
p
1.
2.
2.
p

3.
p
p
f
4.
ppp
f
ppp

5.
p
cresc.
fp
f
fz
6.
col Pedale
fp
pp
fff
mf
p

7.
pp
mf
p
8.

17 German Dances

(Ländler)

Op. Posth.
D 366

fz
p
p
4.
mf
cresc.
p
decresc.
pp
5.
fp
fp
pp

6.
p
fz
fz
p
fz
fz
p
7.
8
fz
fz
8
8.
p

9.
f
p
10.
p
cresc.
f
fz
ff

11.
1.
2.
12.
p
pp
cresc.
pp
13.
p
tr
tr
mf

p
14.
1.
2.
15.
fp

16.
17.
p
mf
p

German Dance and 17 Ländler

D 139

sf
sf
sf
sf
sf
sf
Fine
TRIO
pp
sf
sf
sf
sf
sf
sf
f
sf
sf
ff
sf
sf
pp sf
sf
sf
sf
sf
sf
1.
2.
D. C.

Ländler

3.
p
sf
f
mf
4.
p
mf
5.
dolce
6.
p

7.
8.

9.
10.
p
sf
f
f
p
f
p
8
8
8

11.
p
sf
tr
f
12.
3

13.
14.
p
f

15.
p
16.
p
8
mf
8
17.
f

8 Ländler

D 681

3.
p
f
4.
f
p
f
p
(Ped.)
(senza Ped.)
5.
p
fz
fz

6.
mf
7.
p
f
8.
f

12 Viennese German Dances

D 128

p
3.

4.
ff
5.
ff
p
f
pp
ff

p
6.
ff
ff

7.
dolce
f
8.
p
1.
2.

1.
2.
9.
ff
fz
fz
p
f

10.

11.
f
12.
f

6 German Dances

D 970

4.
5.
6.
tr
8
tr

3 German Dances

D 971

mf
3.
mf
1.
2.
ff
mf

3 German Dances

D 972

3 German Dances

D 973

mf
1.
2.
3.
p
fz
p
fz
p
mf
pp
f
fz
p
fp

2 German Dances

D 974

2 German Dances

D 769

German Dances

D 722

German Dance

D 975

6 German Dances

D 820

pp
mf
sfp
mf
fp
fp
f
8
fz
p
cresc.
3.
cresc.
decresc.
fz
pp

mf
fp
fp
f
fz
p
cresc.
fz
p
4.
staccato
mf
fz
fz
fz
fz
ffz
p
staccato
mf
fz
fz
fz
fz
ffz
p
ff
fz
p
ff
ff

5.
pp
cresc.
fzp
ff
fz
fz
fz
p
fz
fp
staccato
mf
fz
fz
fz
fz
ffz
p
mf
staccato
fz
fz
fz
fz
ffz
p
ff
fz
p
ff
ff

6.
legato
pp
f
pp
f
staccato
mf
fz
fz
fz
fz
ffz
p
mf
staccato
fz
fz
fz
fz
ffz
p
ff
fz
p
ff
ff

2 German Dances

D 841

German Dance and Ecossaise

D 643

Galop and 8 Ecossaises

Galop

D 735

Ecossaises

4.
p
f
p
f
5.
f
p
ff
6.
p

8
f
7.
p
8
8
8
ff
8.
p
f
fp

3 Ecossaises

D 816

Ecossaise

D 158

11 Ecossaises

D 781

3.
p
fp
fp
1.
2.
f
fz
fz
fz
fz
4.
p
f
fz
fz
fz
p
5.
p
ff
fz
fz

6.
p
ff
f
fz
ff
7.
ff
fz
p
1.
2.
ff
mf
fz
mf
fz
ff
8.
p
f
fz
fz cresc.
fz
ff
fz

9.
p
10.
mf
f
cresc.
ffz
11.
ff
fz
fz
p
ff
fz

8 Ecossaises

D 977

3.
cresc.
fz
fz
fz
fz
4.
f
p
cresc.
f
5.
p
f
f
mf

6.
p
cresc.
f
7.
cresc.
8.
f
mf
1.
2.

6 Ecossaises

D 421

4.
p
cresc.
ff
5.
p
6.
mf

5 Ecossaises

D 697

3.
mf
f
4.
fz
ffz
fp
ff
5.
fp
tr
p
1.
2.

12 Minuets

Op. Posth.
D 41

2.
ff
ff
p
f
Fine
Trio
p
stacc.
cresc.
f
p
pp
legato
D. C. al Fine

3.
f
p
cresc.
non legato
tr
f
sempre f
ff
Fine
Trio
p
mf
tr
mf
p
Da Capo al Fine

4.
cresc.
Fine
Trio
cresc.
Da Capo al Fine

5.
f
p
f
p
ten.
f
p
f
ff
ten.
f
p
Fine
Trio
dolce
mf
pp
p
Da Capo al Fine

6.
ff
cresc.
pesante
p
f
sf Fine
Trio
p
mf
cresc.
f p
Da Capo al Fine

7.
f
p
cresc.
f
cresc.
ff
Fine
Trio
p
mf
f
dimin.
pp
p
Da Capo al Fine

8.
Trio
cresc.
Fine
Da Capo al Fine

9.
tr
f
p
mf
ff
Fine
Trio
cresc.
pp
sf
Da Capo al Fine

10.
f
p
cresc.
f
p
cresc.
f
cresc.
Fine
Trio
p
mf
dimin.
p
Da Capo al Fine

11
f
p
Fine
Trio
pp
p
poco cresc.
pp
Da Capo al Fine

12.
p
cresc.
cresc.
f
p
f
Fine
Trio
pp
mf
p
cresc.
f
pp
mf
Da Capo al Fine

Minuet

D 335

Da Capo
Trio II
fz
fz
fz
fz
fz
fz
fz
fz
fz
fz
fz
Da Capo

Minuet

2 Minuets

D 380

2nd time to Trio II
Trio I
Menuetto da capo
Trio II
Menuetto da capo

Minuet

D 600

Graz Galop

D 925

mf
p
mf
cresc.
ff
fz
fz
p
cresc.
f
mf
cresc.
ff
fz
fz

Trio

"to be regarded as the lost son of a minuet"

D 610

Variation on a Waltz by Anton Diabelli

D 718